For my children, Henry and Nora —G.B.

This book is dedicated to all the children who will love to read Gwendolyn Brooks's delightful poems over and over. —F.R.

BRONZEVILLE
Boys and Girls

By Gwendolyn Brooks
Illustrated by Faith Ringgold

HarperCollins*Publishers* Amistad

c o n t

ents

Mexie and Bridie

A tiny tea-party
Is happening today.
Pink cakes, and nuts and bon-bons on
A tiny, shiny tray.

It's out within the weather,
Beneath the clouds and sun.
And pausing ants have peeked upon,
As birds and God have done.

Mexie's in her white dress,
And Bridie's in her brown.
There are no finer Ladies
Tea-ing in the town.

5

Val

When grown-ups at parties are laughing,
I do not like the sound.
It doesn't have any frosting.
It doesn't go up from the ground.

So when my Daddy chased me
Away from the bend in the stair,
With a "Get about your business!"
I didn't really care.

I'd rather be in the basement.
I'd rather be outside.
I'd rather get my bicycle
And ride.

Timmy and Tawanda

It is a marvelous thing and all
When aunts and uncles come to call.
For when our kin arrive (all dressed,
On Sunday, in their Sunday-best)
We two are almost quite forgot!
We two are free to plan and plot.
Free to raid Mom's powder jar;
Free to tackle Dad's cigar
And scatter ashes near and far;
Free to plunder apple juice;
Let our leaping Rover loose.
Lots of lovely things we two
Plot and plan and quickly do
When aunts and uncles come to call,
And rest their wraps in the outer hall.

Narcissa

Some of the girls are playing jacks.
Some are playing ball.
But small Narcissa is not playing
Anything at all.

Small Narcissa sits upon
A brick in her back yard
And looks at tiger-lilies,
And shakes her pigtails hard.

First she is an ancient queen
In pomp and purple veil.
Soon she is a singing wind.
And, next, a nightingale.

How fine to be Narcissa,
A-changing like all that!
While sitting still, as still, as still
As anyone ever sat!

Andre

I had a dream last night. I dreamed
I had to pick a Mother out.
I had to choose a Father too.
At first, I wondered what to do,
There were so many there, it seemed,
Short and tall and thin and stout.

But just before I sprang awake,
I knew what parents I would take.

And *this* surprised and made me glad:
They were the ones I always had!

Keziah

I have a secret place to go.
Not anyone may know.

And sometimes when the wind is rough
I cannot get there fast enough.

And sometimes when my mother
Is scolding my big brother,

My secret place, it seems to me,
Is quite the only place to be.

Charles

Sick-times, you go inside yourself,
And scarce can come away.
You sit and look outside yourself
At people passing by.

Cynthia in the Snow

It SUSHES.
It hushes
The loudness in the road.
It flitter-twitters,
And laughs away from me.
It laughs a lovely whiteness,
And whitely whirs away,
To be
Some otherwhere,
Still white as milk or shirts.
So beautiful it hurts.

John, Who Is Poor

Oh, little children, be good to John!—
Who lives so lone and alone.
Whose Mama must hurry to toil all day.
Whose Papa is dead and done.

Give him a berry, boys, when you may,
And, girls, some mint when you can.
And do not ask when his hunger will end,
Nor yet when it began.

Paulette

What good is sun
If I can't run?

"You're eight, and ready
To be a lady."

That is what my Mama says.
She is right again, I guess.

But there! I saw a squirrel fly
Where it is secret, green, and high.

And there! Those ants are bustling brown,
And I require to chase them down!

What good is sun
If I can't run?

15

Rudolph Is Tired of the City

These buildings are too close to me.
I'd like to PUSH away.
I'd like to live in the country,
And spread my arms all day.

I'd like to spread my breath out, too—
As farmers' sons and daughters do.

I'd tend the cows and chickens.
I'd do the other chores.
Then, all the hours left I'd go
A-SPREADING out-of-doors.

16

Eppie

A little girl wants something
That's perfectly her own.

Something that she can talk about
On the telephone.

Or in the classroom (softly,
And knowing that she shouldn't!)—

Or at the movies, to her chum,
(Although she mostly wouldn't
Disturb a nervous neighbor!)—

Or maybe to her mother.

Something to talk about, and put
Into a box, or other
"Own-place": perhaps a drawer,
Beneath the hankies and
Pink camisole, best anklets,
Sash with the satin band.

Ella

Beauty has a coldness
That keeps you very warm.
"If I run out to see the clouds,
That will be no harm!"

So Ella left her oatmeal
And fleecy coat behind
And ran into the winter
Where there were clouds to find.

Mother-dear went following,
But reprimand was mild.
She knew that clouds taste better than
Oats to a little child.

Dave

My baby sister will be fat.
Oh, there is no avoiding that.

For, when she cries,
To dry her eyes
I always pop
A chocolate-drop
Into her pretty mouth. Since this
Soothes her faster than a kiss.

Luther and Breck

In England, there were castles.
Here, there never are.
And anciently were knights so brave,
Off to bold deeds afar,
And coming back to long high halls
So stony, so austere!
These little boys care nothing for
Their wooden walls of HERE.

Much rather mount a noble steed
And speed to save the Queen;
To chop, in dreadful grottoes,
Dragons never seen.

Michael Is Afraid of the Storm

Lightning is angry in the night.
Thunder spanks our house.
Rain is hating our old elm—
It punishes the boughs.

Now, I am next to nine years old,
And crying's not for me.
But if I touch my mother's hand,
Perhaps no one will see.

And if I keep herself in sight—
Follow her busy dress—
No one will notice my wild eye.
No one will laugh, I guess.

Eldora, who Is Rich

"A RICH girl moved in there," they said.
And thought to find a golden head,
Almost, with diamond ears and eyes!
But soon there came a nice surprise.
They saw a child run out to see
Themselves. She yelled, "Please play with me!"
And brought her doll, and skipped, and smiled,
Like any other little child.

Beulah at Church

You have to be just clean, you know,
You have to be just straight.
No door-screen dust upon your nose,
No rust from the iron grate.

No rust, either, from the fire-tongs,
With which you may like to play.
And you should not be loud at all,
Nor even very gay;

But only hold your song-book—so!—
With the big people closing you in,
And the organ-sound and the sermon
Washing you clean of sin.

I do not want to stay away.
I do not think I should.
Something there surprises me:
It feels good to be good.

Skipper

I looked in the fish-glass,
And what did I see.
A pale little gold fish
Looked sadly at me.
At the base of the bowl,
So still, he was lying.
"Are you dead, little fish?"
"Oh, no! But I'm dying."
I gave him fresh water
And the best of fish food—
But it was too late.
I did him no good.
I buried him by
Our old garden tree.
Our old garden tree
Will protect him for me.

Robert, Who Is Often a Stranger to Himself

Do you ever look in the looking-glass
And see a stranger there?
A child you know and do not know,
Wearing what you wear?

Lyle

Tree won't pack his bag and go.
Tree won't go away.
In his first and favorite home
Tree shall stay and stay.

Once I liked a little home.
Then I liked another.
I've waved Good-bye to seven homes.
And so have Pops and Mother.

But tree may stay, so stout and straight,
And never have to move,
As I, as Pops, as Mother,
From land he learned to love.

Nora

I was not sleeping when Brother said
"Good-bye!" and laughed, and teased my head;
And went, like rockets, out of the door,
As he has done most days before.

But it was fun to curl between
The white warm sheets, and not be seen,

And stay, a minute more, alone,
Keeping myself for my very own.

Mirthine at the Party

"Was I next-to-pretty,"
Said Midge to Maggie Mae,
"I'd wear those beads and bangles
That Mirthine wears today."

"And I, I'd laugh like Mirthine,
And, like Mirthine, be proud,
Was I next-to-pretty,"
Maggie Mae avowed.

Mirthine-next-to-pretty
At school, without her gay
Giggles, beads and bangles, looks
Like Midge and Maggie Mae.

Maurice

Maurice must move away
Into another town.
And this it is that keeps him somer-
Saulting like a clown!
Maurice importantly
PEACOCKS up and down.

Till bigly it occurs to him
(It hits him like a slam)
He can pack balls and cowboy belts,
Not Bill and Hess and Sam.

De Koven

You are a dancy little thing,
You are a rascal, star!
You seem to be so near to me,
And yet you are so far.

If I could get you in my hands
You'd never get away.
I'd keep you with me always.
You'd shine both night and day.

Gertrude

When I hear Marian Anderson sing,
I am a STUFFless kind of thing.

Heart is like the flying air.
I cannot find it anywhere.

Fingers tingle. I am cold
And warm and young and very old.

But, most, I am a STUFFless thing
When I hear Marian Anderson sing.

Marie Lucille

That clock is ticking
Me away!
The me that only
Yesterday
Ate peanuts, jam and
Licorice
Is gone already.
And this is
'Cause nothing's putting
Back, each day,
The me that clock is
Ticking away.

Cheryl's Mootsie

My Mootsie sits an HOUR, about!—
And stiffly stares around,
Living her lovely little life
With scarcely any sound.

I want to wrap myself in fur,
And be a hushed-up thing.
(Except, I'd chase a mouse, or push,
Sometimes, a ball of string.)

Jim

There never was a nicer boy
Than Mrs. Jackson's Jim.
The sun should drop its greatest gold
On him.
Because, when Mother-dear was sick,
He brought her cocoa in.
And brought her broth, and brought her bread.
And brought her medicine.
And, tipping, tidied up her room.
And would not let her see
He missed his game of baseball
Terribly.

Eunice in the Evening

What is so nice in the dining room
Is—Everybody's There!
Daddy on the long settee—
A child in every chair—
Mama pouring cocoa in
The little cups of blue.
(And each of us has leave to take
A ginger cookie, too.)

Vern

When walking in a tiny rain
Across the vacant lot,
A pup's a good companion—
If a pup you've got.

And when you've had a scold,
And no one loves you very,
And you cannot be merry,
A pup will let you look at him,
And even let you hold
His little wiggly warmness—

And let you snuggle down beside.
Nor mock the tears you have to hide.

Otto

It's Christmas Day. I did not get
The presents that I hoped for. Yet,
It is not nice to frown or fret.

To frown or fret would not be fair.
My Dad must never know I care
It's hard enough for him to bear.

Tommy

I put a seed into the ground
And said, "I'll watch it grow."
I watered it and cared for it
As well as I could know.

One day I walked in my back yard,
And oh, what did I see!
My seed had popped itself right out,
Without consulting me.

The Admiration of Willie

Grown folks are wise
About tying ties
And baking cakes
And chasing aches,
Building walls
And finding balls
And making planes
And cars and trains—
And kissing children into bed
After their prayers are said.

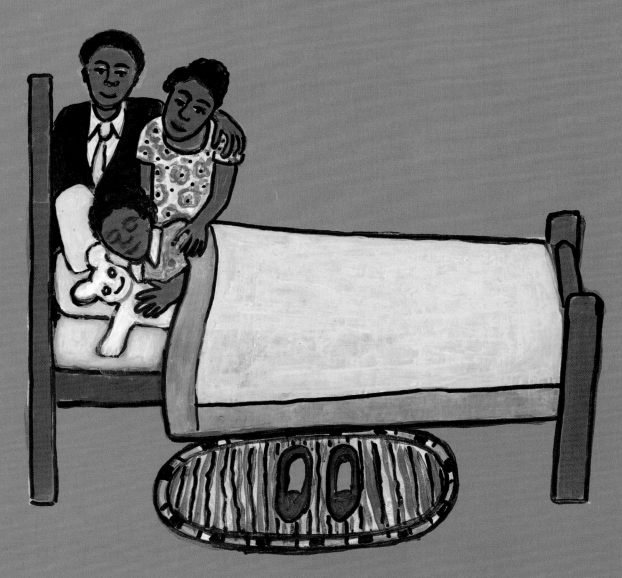

About *Bronzeville Boys and Girls*

Gwendolyn Brooks

In 1956, Gwendolyn Brooks created a collection of poems that celebrated the joy, beauty, imagination, and freedom of childhood. She reminded us that whether we live in the Bronzeville section of Chicago or any other neighborhood, childhood is universal in its richness of emotions and new experiences. We are all Bronzeville boys and girls: We are Mexie and Bridie having a tea party; we are Cynthia playing in the snow; we are Michael holding his mother's hand during the storm; we are Vern walking the dog in the rain. Nora Brooks Blakely, the author's daughter, says the poems are beloved "because these little pieces of life are a 'that's me!' for children and a push of the 'recall' button for adults. Who hasn't pondered their parents, felt insecure around a special girl or boy, wanted to be someplace they are not? *Bronzeville Boys and Girls* connects with our thens and our nows."

■   ■   ■

What a pleasure it was to illustrate these delightful poems. Children will love to read them over and over. I know I did. Each poem introduces a very special boy or girl character. Some of them I knew quite well from my own childhood, growing up in Harlem in the 1930s. Others were new but valued acquaintances. While creating the illustrations, I quickly lost myself in the period and the place as if I, too, were a Bronzeville boy or girl. —Faith Ringgold

Faith Ringgold